LIVING IN THE

BEAST

SYSTEM

"EXPOSING THE DRAGON'S HIDDEN METHODICAL
AGENDA IN THE LAST DAYS"

DORIS L. GRIER

DEDICATION

My life is my dedication to God. I could never repay him for what he has done and is doing in my life.

I'm thankful for my beautiful daughter Danielle; you are everything I wanted in a daughter and more.

To my sister Cheryl, thank you for being a light in my world and many others.

TABLE OF CONTENTS

INTRODUCTION

LUKE 4:5-7

The Devil led him up to a prominent place and showed him all the world's kingdoms instantly. And he said to him, "I will give you all their authority and splendor; it has been given to me, and I can give it to anyone I want to. If you worship me, it will all be yours

At an early age, God spoke to me about the end times through visions, conversations, and expressing that The Great Tribulation would happen soon during my lifetime. While aware of this revelation, my understanding was not grasping the seriousness of what God brought to me because I tried to place my mind in a state of dissociation. This state of dissociation brought me nothing but misery. As misery consumed my heart, I saw that the dreams that God had revealed to me were not so much of a distant reality but a present one. His plans, visions, and unfailing words unfurled before me. My mind eventually had to accept his word, not my false sense of truth.

After I shed many tears of doubt and sorrow for humanity, God taught me more about the end times. As our relationship grew more robust, the questions grew more profound, and the responses increased more intensely. I had to take away my reasoning and logic to understand God's picture because I knew my reason and logic meant nothing compared to the all-knowing God.

God knows that the people of this world are stuck in many levels of deception. This deception has such a firm hold on the inhabitants of planet earth. Satan, of course, created this deception. We are not strangers to his deceptive tactics: this has happened to humanity since the beginning. He has repeatedly convinced us to go against God's word. This rebellious behavior has led us down the road of hardship and pain. Satan also referred to as the Dragon in **(Revelation 12:9),** is a character full of manipulation and deception. The Book of Revelation says that, during the end times, the Dragon will put a system in place to manipulate many, as they will soon bow down to him. The Dragon knows the power behind free will. In the end, some would exercise their free will and follow God. Ultimately, we also have those who will exercise free will and follow the Dragon. Also, we have a group of people who still need to learn they are currently being guided and dictated by the Dragon, who will lead them into a fiery abyss.

A system is laid in place for the Dragon to gain control of people unknowingly. This systematic method, derived from the Dragon, will be built on many illusions and lies derived from the art of manipulation.

"Manipulation (v): to control or play upon by artful, unfair, or insidious means, especially to one's advantage. "

The Dragon's thoughts and acts of manipulation upon us are merely a form of sick entertainment for him. His joy comes from us dancing across a stage. This stage that he watches us dance and frolic upon is called Earth. His kingdom is upon this planet called "Earth." He watches closely as we unwittingly indulge in the venoms of this world.

Our unawareness brings us closer to our last meal as if we were on death row. We gorge on the feast from the enemy's table while he smirks with accomplishment. His smirk is there because he will never tell the truth about who we are, what we are doing, and the tasteless venom we feast on at his dinner table. He hides behind the walls of deception, walls that he constructed.

For the Dragon will never tell the truth. He wants your soul to perish like his, for he is pretty miserable, and so shall we be soon when we bow down to him because we have eaten at his table and feasted on deceit. He will deceive many. It doesn't matter your race, religion, culture, economic status, or if you are a prominent representative of society. He could not care less of who you are: your soul is fair game to him. Your soul is so vital that he designed a system that would and could condemn your soul to Hell if you are a part of it.

Let's picture the Dragon system as a factory that produces car parts. For a factory to run effectively and smoothly, there has to be an intricate system in place. It would be best if you had people in a place like your machinist, production worker, and boss. Underneath the Dragon will be many beasts, operating and working for him to complete his mission of total control of the human race.

There are so many people in this world currently promoting the beast system. These are your politicians, church leaders, celebrities, and wealthy individuals. He knows his time is running out, but he's manipulating his workers to believe they would share eternal power or success with him, which is just another lie. Lies are needed to get his puppets to dance for him.

Sometimes I would ask myself, why can't people see the deception? I began finding that when people reject Christ, they automatically forfeit their rights to understand the truth and see beyond worldly things.

Another reason why people can't see this deception is that the world has normalized this dysfunction. By accepting this normalization as a standard way of living, we have gotten used to this demonically oppressed system. If only many people could and would understand that Christ has overcome the world, that he can see through the lies and gives the insight to help us cope with the world's troubles. The world has rejected Christ before.

The truth about this world underneath the dragon system and the human race is icy and gloomy, especially for those in Christ who watch as the Dragon implements this beast system, as it grows stronger daily. It's almost like a horror film you don't want to watch, but you can't look away. As a people and human race, we suffer in this world of wickedness. As we suffer in this world, our soul cries out. We are stressed out, unsure about our future and our kids" future, and somehow, we keep looking down or over our shoulders because we feel some impending doom that is about to come our way. Our stress levels continuously seem to climb. It's like we're climbing an unsteady ladder; the farther we go up, the more; our anxieties rise.

Underneath this beast system, many people are trying to cope in the best way possible. We all have different coping mechanisms that work best for us. One type of coping mechanism that works for all of us is technology. Technology has given us the ability to escape. Using technology as escapism has given us a way to cope with the harsh world. When plugged into our devices, we become unplugged from the world. The sound of the earth-cries begins to fade away. A false reality seeps in as the actual reality seeps out.

It is disheartening at times that we are living in the end, and this truth is brutal for many people to understand; it's a burden too hard to bear. The Dragon knows we are distracted, depressed, and consumed with our issues to care about what's happening around us. This truth about the end Times is hard to swallow; indulging in escapism is our lifeline, giving us a sense of normalcy in a not-so-normal world.

My office calls me to bring awareness about the lies and the manipulation of the Dragon underneath his system. It's time to start informing people about the beast system and how we exchanged lies for truth in this last hour. I will tell many about this beast system as the end times continuously approach. So many events are about to occur during these end times. It is time to expose the Dragon's agenda and the people that promote it. I pray that you receive this information that you're about to read. The information I will give you might be very unsettling, but it is very informative and detailed. God gave this information to me to give to you to enlighten you, the reader. It's time to expose the Dragon underneath the beast system and show you the levels of his evil and the depth of his lies. May God grant you the wisdom and the mercy to come out of this treacherous beast system. I pray you will recover but be well-removed from this sophisticated methodical agenda and stop adopting the world's ways.

CHAPTER 1
TWO WORLDS

The idea or thought that another type of world exists other than ours may seem quite bizarre to most. Imagine a world where everything that exists is spiritual; when I was unsaved and living in the world, I wouldn't even entertain any thoughts about the spiritual world. The reason why I wouldn't invite any of these thoughts wasn't that I didn't believe that another world exists. It was because I couldn't understand something I couldn't witness. How could I ever believe in something I had never seen before?

We have all heard the phrase "Seeing is believing"; behind this old monotonous cliche, there is some truth. Most people rely on experience to teach them because experience brings a form of understanding at many different levels of degrees.

One must gain a spiritual mindset through Christ our Lord Jesus Christ to understand the end times. The reason why it's so hard for many theologians to dissect and understand the Bible, especially the Book of Revelation, is because they rely on self-knowledge. A type of self-knowledge gained through education. God is all-knowing and can reveal things about the spirit world that is unknown to man. Engulfed in our world, we can't imagine another world out there, but there is one that significantly impacts our world.

I recall many nights as a child when I would gaze aimlessly at the night sky. So many thoughts filled my mind as my child's eyes feasted on the mesmerizing, velvety blue sky. My intrusive thoughts often told me I was far away from home or a world other than mine. As a child, it is hard to explain or express my emotions of feeling like a foreigner in an unknown-but-known land.

I held back my intrusive thoughts and feelings because I felt that no one would be able to understand me, and I was afraid that they were also judging me and making me feel weirder than I already felt. I couldn't prove that another world did exist, but I knew it was something out there that was so much greater than me or anyone else. As I grew older, the unknown alternate world faded out as the physical world began to overshadow me.

As I entered my adult years and accepted God, I began learning about the Bible. I realized that my far-away-from-home feeling as a youth was utterly ordinary. (I Peter 2:11) states that believers are only visitors here for a short time. I began to see that life here on Earth was only temporary, and when we experience a physical death on Earth, we are then alive in the spirit world. During this time, God began revealing things about his world to me. I also had to learn about the influence of Satan on this world.

We must first learn about the spiritual world to fully grasp or understand the things happening today. We must remember this first to accept and face the things that will happen to us in the future.

What is the Spiritual World?

The spiritual world is a world not easily seen. People don't exist in this world; only spiritual beings, angels, and demons exist. People have encountered them through an experience with or through God; some state they have entered or seen this world through drug usage, witchcraft, and other practices.

Where is God in the Spiritual World?

God is dominion over everyone and everything. God isn't restricted by time, space, or matter. He is omnipresent and omnipotent. God is a spiritual being who created us and our world with his thoughts and desires **(Genesis 1:1)**. God exists in this world, his world, and many others.

Saint John receives a vision from God.

St. John, the author of the Book of Revelation, gives us a frightening and enlightening account of the end times in the spiritual and earthly realm while at Patmos Island due to Christian persecution. St. John's insight into the beast's plans for many during these times is remarkable, and the prophecy will be unmatched in terms of even history's most vivid, explosive.

Biblical Spiritual encounters

Several people in the Bible had many revelations and encounter with the spiritual world. Elijah was taken away to heaven in a fiery chariot **(2 Kings 2:11)**. King Belshazzar received a message from God about his kingdom from the fingers of a human hand that started writing on the wall **(Daniel 5:5)**. Jesus would often tell his disciples about the Kingdom of Heaven **(John 14:2),** and the plans he has for his children in the afterlife.

EVIL SPIRITUAL CEREMONY IN THE LAST DAYS

Round about seven years ago, God gave me this vision about a wicked ceremony that was taking place in the spiritual realm, a demonic ritual presented by Satan and his leaders. I was in the middle of a garden that looked like a maze. The park was lavish and pleasing to the eye, with immaculate beauty. I could see at a distance people walking into a building. The people had crowns on their heads with many beautiful flowers.

I decided to get a closer look because the image of the building and the beauty of the people was very compelling and enchanting. It looked as if a wedding ceremony was about to take place. As I walked closer, I noticed the door attended to by someone in heavy armor on a horse. As I got closer and closer to the building, I began to realize I'd made a big mistake by coming here. I began to feel a heavy demonic presence all around me, and all those once-beautiful people now had the faces of demonic entities.

I saw other people, like me, who this place's floral beauty had lured. I tried to warn them that it was a trap cause, somehow, I knew they were being led to death. I then notice these horrid-looking demonic entities start watching me intensely. They had razor-sharp teeth, droopy eyes, and deformed bodies. They began to run toward me, I ran so fast to escape them, but they caught up with me. One demonic thing pulled out a large knife and was about to stab me, but his hand froze in midair as soon as it was about to strike me. The demonic entity was angry he couldn't kill me because I was a Saint of God.

I was intrigued by all the symbolism when I awoke from this vision. It symbolizes the world that looks pleasing and beautiful to many people on Earth. But living in the world, and pleasing the world, will only lead you down a path of death. One of Satan's manipulation tactics is to make everything appear beautiful and pleasing to the eye.

The Devil and his leaders are in Hell celebrating your death as if it was a wedding because they know they have gained your soul.

These things are taking place in the Spirit World. If we look at the world and see the projections of what is good and correct, we see it is in complete opposition to God's word. To think that the Devil and demonic entities are celebrating that your soul will go to Hell seems unrealistic. No matter how cruel it is, it does not take away the fact that it is the truth. There is nothing new underneath the sun. Many demonic spirituals or rituals are done on Earth to increase the level of demonic activity on Earth.

SACRIFICING CHILDREN

Sacrificing children is a practice that is done today in the physical world. To please Satan, like in the Old Testament days of Baal and Molech

(Leviticus 18:21, Deuteronomy 12:31, Ezekiel 16:20-21)

OPENING PORTALS

God gave me a vision about a year ago. I was at the old childhood home I grew up in and stepped outside to glance around. I remember seeing a dark, massive Black Horse, remarkably untamed and with a very evil demonic presence. The horse was furious as it was untamed. I became so frightened at this image that my knees began to feel like jelly, and I couldn't stand up. I had to convince myself to go back to my home. In my childhood home, I looked at the sky and saw images of demons with black hoodies like the Grim Reaper. There were so many it would be impossible to count them. In my dream, I was afraid and knew this was another level of evil unleashed upon the Earth.

Those who practice the Dragons Kingdom occult are gladly open-ing different realms. They are experimenting with advanced technology given to them by the fallen angels. The goal is to get more demonic activity upon the land so that they can help in the war for the last days.

FALLING ANGELS IN OUR WORLD

The physical manifestation of demons is increasing. Therefore, we can't see or believe everything we see on TV, news, or social media. If we look at many of our world leaders and those who are very influential, we will notice something odd: they do not look normal, like they are trying to fit in. They always seem to have a stiff, rigid look, very emotionless. Have you ever had the experience of watching and studying someone and looking at their mannerisms, and, somehow, they don't seem human?

The fallen angels have possessed our world leaders, giving them the technology we have today. The fallen angels are currently alive and active.

I have seen their true physical form during the last days in visions. Not the state that they present themselves to be. They are very horrible looking and carry a robust, intimidating presence. They were attacking people and targeted Gods Chosen. Seeing them upon our land in their fleshly form was shocking and horrifying for many humans because they didn't think such things or creatures existed. They were powerful, but they couldn't attack those who were in Christ

PUBLIC RITUALS

Wickedness is increasing because of what is happening in the spiritual world, which significantly influences this world. During these last days, we will see sin as we have never seen before. There will be more innocent people sacrificed to the Dragon. These sacrifices will continuously increase. We must be mindful when we go out in public. We must be aware when attending concerts or enormous crowds.

They will start to sacrifice people in front of our faces, but many will still deny the truth of our reality in hopes that the fear might fade away. People will remain astonished at the mere fact that the rituals are out in public now. People's minds won't and can't be able to digest the evil of this degree.

Currently, these rituals are being covered up and explained as if the deaths of many people were just natural acts. It won't be like this for long, though, for they will be upfront and outright with these sacrifices and dare people to do anything. they fear not God and know this is their time to shine for their master, who merely uses them as puppets on a string.

Satan has limited power, and he can't do things without the permission of God **(Revelation 17:17).** Many people would ask why God allows these things to happen to us. But I ask people why we would allow the enemy to steal us away from God's true intent for our lives. See, here's the thing about the Dragon: when you let him in just a little, that still isn't good enough. Despite Satan's influence, God will always be in control. He will try to manipulate you until he fully controls you and the situation, leaving you helpless and with so much deception you will no longer recognize the truth.

The Dragon exists in a world that has some control over ours. If we fool ourselves into thinking that another world doesn't exist, we can't understand the dark forces controlling this world, and our minds are in denial. Denial is the easiest way out. A war is waging between good and evil. This battle is occurring as we continue to live our present lives.

CHAPTER 2
THE DRAGON/BEAST PROFILE

"Know thy enemy" is what God said to me many years back. I was still determining why he would tell me to learn about the Dragon. Learning more about the character of God was way more important to me. I minimized the depth of what God had said unto me. God explained that understanding your opponent's ways is a significant advantage. Things hiding in plain sight become visible when you know the enemy's trick.

God said, "The enemy has the same predictable yet awful behavior."

Many people can't recognize the characteristics of the Dragon because were submerged in a household of dysfunctionality. To see more clearly, we need to step outside the family's dysfunctional behavior and look at the home called planet Earth for what it is worth. To see the Dragon, we must learn his profile. We must dig deep into his identity and discover those helping aid his missions for complete world dominance.

WHO IS THE DRAGON?

In the Book of Revelation, they referred to Satan as "The Dragon" in several verses. A dragon is a ruthless animal that consumes everything in its path and wreaks havoc because it only acts out its true nature.

(Revelation 12:1, Revelation 12:4, Revelation 13:2).

During the great tribulation, The Dragon deceived many people on Earth, causing them to fall away from God and believe in its lies. We know the origin of the Dragon, we know his past life: a life that was once with God, and we are learning about his upcoming future life; the Dragon will have a fate of being cast into an abyss for one thousand years **(Revelation 20:1-3)**

God is in a state of continual time in different aspects, so nobody knows, but God knows the precise amount of time the Dragon will cast away. We can't equate those one thousand years to earth time. For God, 1,000 years can equal up to one day to him.

The Role and Purpose of the Beasts

Since we have already established that the Dragon significantly influences his role during the end times, he is the main character, and the Beast, or Beasts, are like his entourage. The beasts discussed in the Book of Revelation are considered kings/queens with eminent authority in their kingdoms. The Dragon wants his kingdom to reign upon Earth, and he knows the Beasts will fulfill his mission. He trusts them so much that he gives his power and authority **(Revelation 13:2)** to one of the beasts for a little while to act out his mission of complete world domination **(Revelation 13; 11:12)**

These beasts will take action upon the Dragon's command due to promises of a high place or throne in the Dragon's kingdom **(Revelations 17:12)**. Each Beast(s) will fulfill his purpose, to honor the

Dragon and hold a place on his throne of lies. His mission? Many people on Earth will bow down and worship him due to mere fear **(Revelation 13:4)**.

A Beast will control the Anti-Christ.

One of the Beasts, in the end, will possess the Anti-Christ. I had a vision many years ago about a man speaking from a podium, and I could see a demon in Hell talking for him. At that time, I didn't know that God was showing me that it was the Anti-Christ. The Dragon would give his authority to the Antichrist, who the beast possesses to fulfill his purpose **(Revelation 13:2)**

World Leaders Possessed by the Beast

Regardless of our political views, many would like to witness the American government succeed and create a financially and emotionally stable country. Many hold this expectation of hope that we have near our hearts and minds that the government will do what we hire them to do. Some of us stand firm in our hearts that this mere expectation will be our reality someday. Why aren't our world leaders governing us accordingly, taking their oath as government officials very seriously, and remaining truthful to the citizens they represent? In such rays of hope,

Having this type of hope for our government grows dimmer and dimmer every day. As time passes, so do the false promises from our leaders; they have abandoned us!

Many nations" governments have abandoned their people, like the USA. They have let their countries burn into flames to chase and fulfill their self-desires and knowingly fulfill the beast's plan. The Dragon desires everyone to worship and serve him regardless of color, age, and beliefs. The Dragon will give the beast(s) the power to fulfill his will, this massive yet knowing world domination plan. The Dragon will use the beast, who will then possess the leaders of our government, to do hellion acts to their people.

The beast has deceived the world's leaders significantly. He has falsely accused God as the enemy, liar, and deceiver. He has promised them a place in his kingdom, which he knows has a short reign and destroyed **(Revelation 16:10)**. His deception is so strong that those who worship the Dragon believe the lies they spew from his mouth.

Instead of serving the people, our leader has decided to conform to the beast foolishly, allowing him to have complete control over them, causing the government to be under the influence of Satan. The people the Dragon has fooled think the beast's plan is excellent and brilliant. They are not for the sorrows they inflict upon the people of this world. Many leaders in biblical history have inflicted much pain on their citizens due to being heavily influenced by Satan's will or plan. They do care not for the country's citizens or the chaos that will fall upon them

Leaders, worshiping and serving the Devil isn't a foreign practice. King Ahab was one of the many leaders in the Bible who inflicted pain upon his people with his false idol worship. He is considered the worst king in history known to Israel. King Ahab worshiped false idols. As he worships these false idols, he also builds altars unto them **(2 King 21:3)**. King Ahab also sought the approval of false prophets and hated the truth from authenticating ones **(1 Kings 22:8)**. King Ahab brought much distress on Israel **(1 King 18:17-18)**. While under the influence of Baal, King Ahab had a wife that seemed more wicked than him. The king's wife was named Jezebel. She worshipped Baal like him, hated God's true prophets, and ordered that they be slain **(1 King 18:4)**.

This one example highlights the wickedness of the history of one government. Like today's leader, King Ahab, and his wife believe a lie for the truth. Our current government leaders/kings seek advice from false prophets and demonic entities **(Revelation 16:14)**. They know that the end times are here, so they seek counsel from the wicked, for they are corrupt, just like King Ahab and Jezebel.

Leaders of the world know that the great day of the Lord is coming. They won't announce to this world's people that Jesus is about to return; instead, they build secret caves and hide out so when the day does arrive **(Revelation 6:15).** This is a very foolish act, of course, because they can't hide from God. The world's leaders won't be able to escape his judgment upon the Earth and in his presence. I received a vision many years ago about fireballs reigning upon Earth that hit the hidden caves of those who tried to escape God's judgment.

CHAPTER 3
THE MOUTHPIECE

The media is one of many counterparts of "The Beast System. "The Beast uses the media as his mouthpiece to promote foul things such as hatred, division, fear, and a false reality. The mouthpiece is vital to the beast's system; the mouthpiece brings about a mechanism to ensure the beast's message is audible.

Three years ago, I received a vision from God concerning the media. A food supply shortage was happening in America, and people were looting and gunning people down in the streets. My daughter and I had all our windows boarded up, and we saw a man breaking through our boarded window. The stranger was almost through our window, and as he was about to enter our home, he saw us looking at him; this man knew that we would defend ourselves even if it meant we would be violent, and he became afraid of the thought of losing his life and ran away.

My daughter turned on the TV, and every station broadcasted the news about this chaos partaking in the world. As I looked above the reporter's head, I saw a man, or a man-shaped spirit, on a white horse speaking the word of hatred and lies. This man appeared to be angry and full of rage. He talked to the newscaster in the spiritual realm, instigating him to spread more lies.

I decided to flip the stations, and I heard God say

"They continue to spread lies, and keep deception at a high, for the truth doesn't lie in them, my child. They promote what the beast wants. "

As I heard the Lord speak, I knew that we were being played against each other all along, and many believed the lies of the media, and I knew not to trust anything the media says since they are also under the beast's control.

As the media currently remain under the beast's control, we see so much fear being promoted on the news today. The beast wants you to fear many things in the media so that he can gain control of your thoughts and action. To gain control of anyone, you must consume their mind, and everything else will follow. Fear isn't just an emotion; it can also be a state of mind if one allows it. Fear can be a way of life for many who choose to live in it. Fear isn't of God but just another tireless tactic of Satan. The beast knows that many in this world are far from God, so it uses this fear trait to mislead many. Those who discarded God's word have forfeited their right to know the truth. So, an individual without the Holy Spirit is vulnerable to the media's lies, for, without God, you live in a state of deception.

At the End of Time, which is now, the level of deception will be at an all-time high, and Jesus warns us about this **(Matthew 24)**. Those behind the media know that you are easily duped, so they make the news stories sound natural. They use fake news stories to pull on the strings of your emotions, so you can be emotionally involved and not see beyond the lies.

We watch and engage in the media daily, not knowing we are programmed to think how the beast wants us to think or feel. The media teaches you to hate other skin colors different from yours. This is his strategy, and it is working: look under the comment section of social media, news station stories, and video-sharing platforms, and there you have the beast system working perfectly; we are using his platform to speak hatred to one another, creating confusion and chaos.

In October 2021, a former social media employee made accusations that this vast social media platform allegedly put its integrity aside for profitable gain while inciting violence and intentionally ignoring hate speech. They are making a profit from your anger and hate. Your emotions are merely dollar signs to them. Your state of deception has made them more prosperous and allowed them to fulfill the beast's plans of making us hate one another.

The beast speaks through the media, and you are unknowingly, willingly, and proudly listening to him. The beast sits and laughs at you because you have no idea he is speaking and putting these thoughts into your mind. So, the next time you see a news story or read an article, please don't be so quick to jump on the media bandwagon with your thoughts or emotions. Ask God how he feels about this and allow him to reveal to you the truth. Doing this will prevent the deception from being hidden, and God will speak over the beast's lies. So, when you do this, you won't get emotionally entangled with these news stories or articles and will see the truth behind them.

THE DRAGON SINGS

Music can make you feel alive; music can make you cry and recreate old memories. Also, one thing that a lot of people in this world underestimate is the level of sorcery and witchcraft taking place in the music industry. We must remember that Satan oversaw the music in heaven. So, another way that the Dragon speaks is through these musicians of today's world.

As we press ahead towards the End of Times, a lot of the dragon influence is great upon these musicians in the world, and to make him proud and them successful, they cast spells and do rituals over different songs. God told me that a trendy female artist had many spells in her music and would often curse him in her lyrics. Many people play these songs with witchcraft in their cars, their homes, during workouts, and so much more. When worldly people listen to the songs, they think, wow, this is an excellent beat, or this is a great artist, and this song is a classic. So, for them, it's just a great song with a great beat, but those sensitive to God's word can see past beats and identify the word curses in them.

Sometimes we ignore how the Dragon speaks because we seek an audible voice. We must fully recognize that he's talking through those who worship him and follow his orders to taint the music. Therefore, I have consciously decided to avoid radio stations and the top trending artists. Even if we listen to this music in the form of innocence, they're not making it in the state of purity. They're making it by casting spells and a ceremonial type of music to influence the masses. When we sing these songs, we agree with the spirit world. This is so important why we must be careful what we speak over ourselves.

We must also be mindful of "Christian" music because some artists have dived into the secular world. Christian artists are no longer concerned about the worship of him but the worship of themselves.

Music is the Dragon's expertise, so be mindful of what you allow to come into your ears, for it can also agree with your spirit. Music is compelling, and The Dragon knows this because of his first-hand experiences. Therefore, The Dragon has a tight grip on the music industry.

CHAPTER 4
INFILTRATION OF THE CHURCH

Almost everybody knows that the Devil once was an angel. So, we can conclude that the Devil knew God's teaching and significantly understood God's will. So we know that the beast knows how to manipulate God's word because we see that he influenced one-third of God's angels to believe his lies **(Revelation 12:4)**. So, we can't ignore that the Devil and God once had a relationship. Eventually, the relationship went sour because the Devil wanted to overthrow God and turn others against him, deceiving a third of the angels to follow him.

This explosive incident in heaven speaks volumes, revealing Satan's ego problem, envy, and lack of gratitude. He wanted to be God and still does to this day. Satan is trying to run God's churches his way, and people welcome him with open arms. We see this with our own eyes due to the state of the church today.

Ten years ago, I had a vision about the state of God's church. I was walking into a church service and sat down while the pastor was preaching. I was about to be introduced as the guest speaker. However, the pastor told me he decided to go with someone else to speak instead. I looked down at the floor and saw these flyers promoting guest speakers who were Christian celebrities. I felt rejected; I couldn't talk because I wasn't popular. I got up from my chair and was about to leave the church, but a pastor was teaching a sermon in the basement. I was drawn to it by the sound of his teaching.

As I walked closer, I could see people sitting in the chairs, so I decided to walk down the stairs and sit. As I looked around, I could see the walls were like steel, with red glowing lines going through them like human veins. I saw a middle-aged man at the podium speaking on Bible scriptures, and as I looked around me, I could see others very engaged as he talked. As I continued to look at the pastor, his face became that of a horrible demon. His eyes were dark and droopy, his teeth very razor sharp, and he had claws for his fingers.

I could hear him speak all types of evil, but I looked around to realize nobody was seeing or hearing what I was. I got up from my chair and tried to run to the door, but the stairs were missing. I kept jumping up to reach for the door. I looked back at the demon pastor and heard him say, "I'm Satan, and I am currently running God's church. The basement transformed into a pit from Hell while keeping the appearance of a church's beauty.". I jumped higher and harder, trying to escape that pit after hearing the demon speak those awful words. Finally, someone pulled me up on the opposite side of the doorway to help me escape. I remember waking up in dread.

I asked God, "Why are you showing me this?"

God said, "My daughter, I wanted you to see the state of my church and what it has become, to see how Satan influenced those who say they follow me but instead follow Satan's teaching and appalling ways. This here is the state of my church today."

That vision stirred me because I thought how awful it was that Satan significantly influenced the church and how many people turned a blind eye or a deaf ear to him. As these thoughts came into my mind, I also thought about how they could not see him, even in plain sight. So why do people keep missing him? I asked myself. God gave me the answer, plain and simple.

God said, "My church is drenched in the stench of the evil one, so much that they can't smell the deception, the lies, and the manipulation. When you have become a part of something for so long, it's barely recognizable and becomes something natural or normal. Those deep into me, who study, follow my words, and have my decrees at heart, will spot the deception many miles away, for I have helped and guided them to the truth. Many hearts of today's world don't seek the truth but look for acceptance; They forget the only acceptance they will ever need is from me."

It saddened me to hear the words God spoke to me; the truth sometimes is hard to digest, but it also brought delight to my heart. The joy wasn't from the state of the fallen church but from my understanding of right from wrong in today's churches by trusting in my savior's word and studying the Bible.

The chaos of God's churches isn't just limited to church temples or buildings; it is the whole body of Christ. The church is made of many members and many components to function correctly in Christ. (**1 Corinthians 12:12-31**) gives many great verses highlighting outstanding examples of how members of Christ can help God's church or the Body of Christ. These verses also tell us the importance and respect of different roles in Christ along with our common goal and primary purpose, but somehow the church of the current world has lost that purpose or what it means to be a Body of Christ.

The church will be judged first **(1 Peter 4:17)**. In **(Revelation 2-3)** we see seven current churches that God judges according to their works, and we read the outcome of their judgment. These seven Churches are in the First chapters of The Book of Revelation for several reasons. One reason is God wants us to see how he will execute his judgment on today's churches. God wants us to understand how he views the state of the church during the last few days.

Many church leaders overlook that God will judge the church first, or some leaders seem to portray behavior that they won't be judged at all by their reckless unthoughtful actions. Sin is ruining men and women of the cloth. When sin is present, the perception of the truth is very distorted. Some leaders in today's churches are overflowing with corruption. From my observations, I have noticed that sexual perversion is intense in many churches. Pastors have sexual relationships with church members, have kids out of wedlock, and have intimate relationships with the same sex.

Pastors are also exhibiting the spirit of control and manipulation. These church leaders will make you ashamed to question their authority.

How dare you question their leadership and actions—God has ordained them, not you. Many leaders in today's churches exhibit a "know your role" attitude or motto that is displayed widely in the church. Many Pastors don't seek councils from other leaders, they act out of self-will and ignore wise council, yet the Bible states a wise man should seek council **(Proverbs 1:5)**. Pastors are now the judge, lawyer, and jury. Their all-knowing attitude gives pastors the immunity to behave and act as they desire. This behavior is a form of manipulation to gain control over people. False prophets and fake leaders also use this practice.

I have known real Prophetess/Prophets who became ostracized from the church for speaking out against corruption and ungodly traditions. They were cast away for telling the truth. The fear of somebody exposing their secrets to the congregations. They feared people but not God is very mind-boggling to me.

Some church leaders have traded their integrity and forgotten why God has called them. They have exchanged their true purpose for fame, money, **(1 Timothy 6:10)** power, and titles, only to be filled with sorrow. A faithful servant of God must live his life according to the scripture. Some leaders today lack humility and kindness. In **(1 Timothy 3:7-10),** apostle Paul wrote to church leaders to give them a clear understanding of their church roles and the behavior they should exemplify being leaders. Some churches in today's world forget the scriptures and create their law or doctrine.

Almost a decade ago, I attended a church that I was invited to by a family member. This family member lived a homosexual lifestyle, and I thought they were trying to attend church to learn about the power of God and how his word can be effective in their lifestyle to bring about change and restoration. As we arrived at the church, I saw a lot of youths and adults that seemed to participate in this so call "alternate lifestyle," like my family member who invited me to the church.

As I sat in the church pews, I glanced at the stage to check out the pastor during the church announcements, and what I witnessed made my jaw drop to the floor. I saw the pastor up there holding hands with his male companion or boyfriend. At that moment, I knew that I was in a gay church, where they condoned or accepted this lifestyle of same-sex marriages. I'd been naïve thinking churches like this didn't exist.

Concerns flooded my thoughts as I sat in awe, and bewilderment returned to my mind. Later I gathered my thoughts. This church practiced man's decrees, not Jesus Christ, our God's law. If they practiced God's law, they would know that man's way would lead them down a path of destruction and death rather than it will be spiritual or physical

(Proverb 14:12). This is the fate that anyone shall meet if they let sin consume them. The pastor and members of the congregation mind had become reprobate **(Romans 1:27-29)**. They had and have given themselves over to this particular sin of homosexuality.

I realized that the pastor did not know the ramifications of his action. Yet many scriptures are ignored or dismissed because they don't fit humanity's agenda.

The path of self-destruction the church is on will soon end, and we will see it before Christ arrives. Jesus is looking for a spotless church or bride before his return **(Ephesians 5:27) (Revelation 19:17)**. For this to happen, the church must be changed and restored. The restoration of the church, or the preparation for Jesus's bride, is currently happening. As time pushes ahead, we will see many mega-church leaders get exposed. God has given them a chance to repent from their sinful ways, and they reject his opportunity so that he will disclose it to them. Gospel and contemporary artists will be part of the exposure as well. Don't be surprised when God reveals all the immoral practices in local community churches, too.

This type of exposure must occur for the Remnants to take their rightful place in the forefront of God's Churches. The remnants are an elected group of individuals called upon by God to bring restoration to the church and share his truth, among many other things. God's remnants are callous individuals who know that change must happen soon. God's word will be spoken appropriately by the Remnants. The remnants are the leaders of God's true church, not what we are witnessing now. The church has sold out to Satan for some time, and restoration is coming. All this chaos in the church will soon be a thing of the past as we push closer and closer to Jesus's return.

CHAPTER 5
BEAST HEADQUARTERS

A ny significant corporations have a head office and or a headquarters where the most prestigious of the company meets to exercise their voice, opinions, and facts about the company they work for to ensure growth and productivity.

The Dragon and the Beasts have a headquarters where they meet, periodically check in, and get those high ranking like them to do more of their dirty work. The Dragon is in the business of leading many souls away from Christ and has many business partners. They have chosen to set up their headquarters in The United States of America. They know how much the Americans influence the world, and the Dragon took that moment to seize the opportunity to pursue our leaders down a path of destruction. The United States is modern-day Babylon, as discussed in the Book of Revelation.

I know that the Anti-Christ will rise from the USA. To understand the USA is Babylon, one must look at the origin of Babylon in the Old Testament of the Bible **(Genesis 10-11)** and look at the leaders of Babylon during each era. When we cross-examine each Babylon, I find they all had one common denominator. The leaders were full of pride and ego and chose to reject God **(Daniel 3), (Genesis 11:9), (Revelation 18:9)**. The name Babylon isn't just a name, but a spirit: a spirit of corruption and a grandiose God-like complex. **(Revelation 18)**.

In God's Revelation, he gave me a chance to see and understand why John referenced the city that came to incredible ruins as Babylon; John shared this reference since the city of Babylon, throughout the ages, has had a reputation for beauty, growth, and strength. King Nebuchadnezzar was the king of Babylon, a beautiful and formidable empire. So, to get a modern visualization, John had to explain the imagery in his vision that would give an excellent depiction. John was trying to tell us of this power and spirit that modern-day Babylon will possess: a spirit of pride, thirst, and passion for continuously falling into the state of corruption because they have defied God to fulfill their selfish needs.

The USA will try to kill God's Saints.

In modern-day Babylon (America), they will try to destroy and kill off the prophets. Besides their hate for God, they want to kill off the Saints because they want them to be forever silent. The Dragon knows that God speaks through his people, and his Prophets are his mouthpiece. They would like the truth to no longer exist so that they may spread the deceit. Furthermore, Just like in the days of Elijah, when Jezebel killed God's Prophets **(I King 18:4),** The Anti-Christ ordered many prophets to be jailed or beheaded during his reign. Babylon will persecute God's people **(Revelation 17:6)**.

Come Out of Babylon

The beast system's culture is in our country's whole operation. Those who live in America must not partake in its culture. Please don't indulge in the culture of Babylon, for it will lead you straight to Hell! Don't adopt the ways of its culture, for it will consume you like a raging fire and leave no evidence of your destruction because the evil spirits are running rampant and are seeking and waiting for their next victim.

Why is God Judging America?

Modern-day Babylon has its sins piled up **(Revelation 18:5)**. In America, we have thrown many rocks and hidden our hands. We have manipulated many and preyed upon the innocent because we are a nation of strength. The USA is a country that romanticizes the idea we are untouchable. America is home to workers of iniquity and home to many detestable things. God is judging us for the seen and the unseen things. God is a rightful Judge, so for America to be considered so harshly by God means that we deserve it; we receive this judgment according to our works.

CHAPTER 6
LIVING IN THE NEW WORLD ORDER

There are many discussions, books, and various topics on social media about the New World Order. These topics range from when it will arrive to the mastermind(s) behind it. I then realized that most people don't see what's in front of them; instead, they are too busy looking for it. These diabolical debates online bring to mind the old anecdote about the frog and the boiling water. The water's gradual warming of the water doesn't alarm the frog because he has comfortably submerged. This contentment and cluelessness have brought this frog to its demise in minutes. The people of this world are like the frog in so many ways: we will stray away from immediate danger, but when the change is gradual, we will withstand it until it is too late, and, just like the frog, we will be meeting with a demise of our own.

The New World Order isn't in the future; it is now! We watch these changes in the world and sit back and think the new world order will be just one major event that will occur. There are various steps and levels in the New World order. We are currently in the New world order, at which level I can't say, but I know we are in the enemy's waters like a frog in boiling water.

Let's not forget that the dragon/serpent wants to be like God, but everything he touches will be vile and corrupt like him. Instead of the current world, he wants to create a New World, a free world. The idea of a New World order has a world without God; look around you. Can't you see that this world is falling more and more away from the creator? Satan is so envious of God that he will remake God's world since he couldn't create his world. Look at what Satan has done underneath this New World Order.

Broken Households

Today's households are tremendously broken. In a single-family built home, both parents are out of the house and busy working to sustain a livable and constructive environment for their children. When both parents are alive and worn out from their day, they are exhausted, and many can't give their children 100% of the attention they need. Some parents would instead let their children sit in front of a TV or iPad just for a few minutes of peace. This system's distraction and woes have caused many to raise their kids in a society where electronics are growing them.

Promotion of Pedophilia/Sexualization of Children

The normalization of pedophilia is at a high. This sickening behavior is being shoved right into our minds and faces. I had to cancel many subscriptions to significant networks due to the unpalatable fact that they promote a culture of oversexualizing our youth. This media promotion is like a grooming or conditioning process for our minds.

They bring transgender in the classrooms to speak with children about sexuality and create books to promote this agenda. They are trying to pass bills where educators can discuss sexuality in classes. Kids are being pushed into sexual behaviors, and rather than letting them be children, they are forcing these ideas and logic unto today's youth.

Censoring

Many media platforms have already started suppressing many people's concepts that don't align with the views and opinions of those who control the media. I know people whose social media accounts have been banned or suspended because they spoke the truth about this world. Underneath the New world order, censorship is a must for them to control the narrative.

We are Living under constant Tyranny.

We live under the constant pressure of our current government in the United States. We need help with inflation and heavy taxation. Our leaders get more raises while we struggle to put gas in our cars and food on the table. The housing market is thriving for investors. Owning a home feels more like a dream than a reality for many. As rent prices soar, medicine and healthcare costs fall close behind. Our government only regulates things they can profit from and does not handle essential matters that would help the people they have sworn to protect.

Promotion of Gender Confusion

The Dragon is the author of confusion, and today we promote demonic oppression of the mind and dress it up to look like it is something profound. The gender identity crisis, or confusion, has become so widely accepted that people don't believe in the gender that God has made them. God created man and woman, and God drew a line in the sand on the separation of gender. Yet we allow those mentally demonically possessed people or group organizations to spread a false narrative about who we are.

We are God's creation, and the promotion of this demonically oppressed mindset brings us further away from God. The Dragon is aware of what this mindset will cause, so celebrities and the media will promote this because this is another component in the beast system: this promotion of gender confusion, which is just another way to fall further from God's truth. When people become confused about their sex, they will forever be confused about many other life choices and decisions. We welcome the Dragon to have full authority when we omit God's truth.

Many events are unfolding right in front of us, yet we choose to look for other signs. We may look for certain circumstances to define whether we live in this "New World Order." The lack of discernment and the illusionary reality we reside in create room for the Dragon to treat us like the frog and the boiling water; we will only understand the seriousness of our course of actions once it's too late to undo it.

No need to look for the New World order; it's time to start looking for a way out of the "New World Order" and stop giving them what they need to fulfill this mission of a world without God, even though a world without God is impossible. We must pray hard every day to fight against the New World Order.

CHAPTER 7
METHOD OF
DISTRACTIONS

A s we understand the Dragon/Beast(s) more and more, we see this pattern of destruction, confusion, and chaos. For the beast to gain control, it must make the people of the land dependent on them. They want us to make war with each other instead of with them. Distractions are a must to keep up the chaos among us. These distractions allow for them (Dragon/Beast) to keep their eyes off them so we can center our focus on meaningless matters that hold no value or importance in our lives.

Many would not believe that the Dragon is behind this world's chaos. This plot is often the subject in many great mystery novels where nobody suspects a typical person might be the perpetrator. Behind every excellent mystery book, the antagonist is cunning, manipulative, and creative. Sometimes the antagonist is revealed in the early chapters, and sometimes they are displayed at the end. The protagonist is and will always show, even if they try to hide their web of lies and deceit.

Underneath this beast system, the Dragon, the protagonist, must try to remain hidden and blame others while his current agenda works out. The enemy in plain sight—this is one of his most incredible tricks. The Dragon and the Beast want to distract you from them with frivolous and meaningful things that hold no value in the Kingdom of God. Here is a list of distractions to keep your eyes off them:

PROMOTION OF HATRED

Watching the news in America, you would think there are only two races worldwide. The two races would be those who are of African descent and those who are of European descent.

The enemy knows the history between "black" and "White"; both cultures have strained relationships for many years. Since the enemy knows this, he will play upon the insecurity of both cultures. This promotion of hatred and division is very demonic. Those who indulge in such despicable behavior shall not inherit the kingdom of God **(Galatians 5:19-20)**. God does not show favoritism to any nationality **(Acts 10:34-35)**. God shows no partiality **(Romans 2:11)**. God has commanded us to love one another **(Romans 12:10)**.

Four years back, God gave me a vision and showed me that the government hires African Americans and Caucasian individuals to commit crimes. The government promises them money and sworn protection if they commit violent acts to accomplish their agenda to promote hate. The people they hire to convince them to do these sick crimes get killed by them, or they frame an innocent individual.

SLAVERY

The federal minimum wage is $7.65 an hour in America. Many hardworking Americans can't afford to keep food on the table and keep their cars running on the road simultaneously. Wages have increased a bit, but the cost of living has almost doubled. People are exhausted from working and barely making ends meet. Many are too distracted to hear the truth about the world because it can be overbearing, so many people indulge in many other things. Who has time to focus on other matters when busy busting their tails to provide for their families?

Whoever implemented this word schedule system in America and many other countries built it to make the upper class wealthier. Instead of teaching us to be innovators and creating wealth for ourselves. They made us feel like going to college and getting an education to work for someone else is the American dream; while many drown in college debt, they are still in misery at their jobs, regardless of how much they make. We are nothing but merely modern-day slave laborers. We are simply in bondage to a system that uses our bodies to create wealth for them.

Hard work isn't everything, and the things we purchase with this hard work mean nothing in the End **(Ecclesiastes 2:11).** We gain material things, but what has this busy world done to our spirit? Work is necessary, but this system is more about exploiting those in "lower places" or on the bottom of the world's totem pole. This horrible system pulls us away from living life. Often, I find myself just in survival mode when I should be living life instead and not trying to compete with it. Being so consumed with this work system, what time do we have to question a system built on greed? We are in debt to everything that we think is a convenience.

Right Wing / Left Wing

When I see people arguing on social media or at the dinner table about Democratic Party vs. the Republican Party, I act out an intense eye roll in my mind. I began thinking about the prominent religious figures active during Jesus' ministry. They often judge and critique Jesus when their lives are full of hypocrisy. Jesus called the Pharisees out for crooked ways **(Matthew 23:1-39)**, explaining how they put a show on for others but were full of corruption. The Sadducees even tried to tell Jesus there were no such things as a resurrection **(Matthew 22:23)**. They even rejected angels and matters of the spirit world **(Acts 23:8).**

The Pharisees and Sadducees are much like our modern political groups. They shared different opinions, but they both opposed God's word. Our modern-day political groups present this same behavior as ancient-day religious and government figures. When we consume ourselves with groups, religion, or government officials and try to convince others that one party is more corrupt than the other, we get consumed in opinion rather than fact. People who get into heated debates about political parties don't understand the spiritual aspect when dealing with politics during the end times.

Today, the beast dictates the world government, and politicians seek the beast out for answers. In the Bible, Saul was a King, and Kings were the head of government officials. Saul sought out the spirit of Samuel at the time through a medium for advice about his kingdom that would soon come to ruins because he felt the powerful silence of God. **(1 Samuel 28 1:20)** Saul is an example of what desperate measures our leaders will go to get a prophecy about "their" kingdoms.

We are so obsessed with the world's politics that we must focus on what matters. As we lose focus, we center our minds on meaningless matters. These political confusions, distractions, and divisions are another tactic of the Dragon to keep eyes off him, so he can do what he does best. When you save the focus on God, your soul will emerge from those distractions, and the Christ in you will make you aware of the distraction.

CHAPTER 8
GLOBAL CHAOS

A bout ten years ago, I received a vision about the falling of many nations during the end. I saw a map of the world from a bird's eye view, and I saw one continent after another crumble like a demolished building, and I could see the smoke filling the sky. When I saw the first continent destroyed, I was in fear, and I witnessed many other continents fall after the first one. This collapsing of the continents reminded me of the domino effect. I was overflooded with sorrow as I saw what was happening worldwide. **(Revelation 18:20)**.

The vision of the nation's falling aroused my end-time imagination as an adolescent child. I could see the world in my dream like I was looking at a movie play out on the Television, and it looked like a demolition crew had wrecked the world. Everything was out of place: the bodies of water had flooded the land, and mountains moved, the whole world was so messy, but what amazed me was that it was still people on Earth alive, and I could feel his presence come to Earth, and I could remember nothing else after that. I often saw the world and how it would appear when Jesus returned as a young child.

The Antichrist is already here and will rise to power when there is so much turmoil on the Earth, and people will need help and look for answers because he will present as a god who will save the world from this destruction **(2 Thessalonians 2:3-4)**. While we live in this Dragon system, there will be major chaotic events that the Dragon ordained to get people to bow down and worship him.

War on Currency

When people hear the word "war," they may think of military soldiers fighting on the battlefield. War can be on the battlefield, but there are many acts of war. World leaders are intentionally sabotaging the world currency system so that we may fail, and we can depend on the beast currency system. This financial limitation and strain will make it hard for those worldwide to support themselves. Businesses will go under, and the government will buy out others or force them to sell so that the only monopoly will be theirs. Government assistance will be no more. God gave me a vision where many were homeless and getting laid off from work because the American economy had crashed. I saw America's "wealth" fall in seconds, just like it stated in **(Revelation 18:17)**. I saw our country turn into a pile of rubble.

In America, they are lying about why they are constantly raising this imaginary debt ceiling. Our government says we are rising in debt because they must sustain many government-funded programs. I wonder why they left out that they are funding senseless wars, investing money to obtain kickbacks from pharmaceutical companies, and lining their pockets with most of these "funds."

The Dragon/ Beast system uses its platform called the "government" to feed us information about financial debt. The government spreads false information about our financial state for the economic collapse to appear as an unintentional event. This unintentional event is an alibi to cover up their real intentions of ruining this country; the Dragon/Beast and The Government will never work against each other, for they are the same. In (**Matthew 12:25**) Jesus spoke about division and how a divided house can't stand.

Health Pandemic

At the beginning of 2020, we received news of a highly contagious and transmittable virus. This virus was called Covid 19, or coronavirus. This virus brought so much fear and much panic globally. I often would listen to news stories and reports about the dangers of this virus when I heard God telling me to turn off the news and listen only to him because they were full of lies when I turned away from the media. I began to see that this wasn't a virus derived from an animal called a "bat" but a virus that man created. The Covid 19 virus is still alive and present today.

Covid 19, or the coronavirus, is a visible example of chemical warfare among the people of this Earth. Man created this virus because those who call themselves the elite, i.e., leaders, know that the Earth is "overpopulated." This "overpopulated" Earth will soon deplete its resources as time progresses in the next few years. The Covid 19 virus was a way for them to induce population control: they anticipated the death toll to be more than it was. People did lose their lives due to this virus, and some are currently suffering complications from this lab-made virus.

Vaccination Fallen Angel Technology

Doing the COVID-19 pandemic, they push for vaccination throughout the entire world. I asked God numerous times what it is about this vaccination that is so important and why they were making a vaccination to something that they created inside of a lab. For many years I did not get an answer on why they were pushing this COVID-19 vaccination. Recently it has been revealed to me by God that they have used a technology given to them by the fallen angels for the Vaccine.

People are experiencing heart disease, Blood clots, heart attacks, and adult sudden death syndrome. They used this vaccination as an experiment to rewire the human genetic code. Therefore, they push everyone to get vaccinated against this lab-made virus hurriedly. In the future, we will see many deaths and mutations from this virus; the Antichrist is behind this sick experiment. There will be a genetic mutation in the future. I had many visions of zombie-like human figures trying to attack many people. We hid in subways, houses, and other places to escape these zombie-like figures. Genetic Mutation is shortly arriving at our doorsteps.

CHEMTRAILS

For many years I dreamed about a white powdery mist-like substance being sprayed all over the sky. The government and the media try to control the narrative about the Chemtrails, to keep people blinded from the truth. They administer this chemical in the poorest communities. They tried to cover this up and label everyone a conspiracy theorist when people started coming together about this issue. There are so many articles online to disprove Chemtrails is just another "conspiracy" that it makes you think: why try to disprove a fake topic?

There will be another biowarfare coming to us soon. Biowarfare will continue toward the last days as Jesus returns. Why Biowarfare? The people who feel like they are "selected individuals" desire to weed out those beneath them so the Earth can remain sustainable in their sick, demented eyes. Those who create and distribute this type of warfare will be dealt with accordingly by God, who doesn't sleep nor slumber. Please be prepared to endure another Biowarfare!

Cutting off Resources

There will soon be a limitation and a short supply of natural resources underneath the Beast system. Resources are scarce, and the media is trying not to highlight this scarcity. They are buying up all the resources and storing them away. They have purchased much land and prepared safe havens for themselves because of greed **(Revelation 6:15-16)**. That's why you won't be able to buy or sell without the beast's permission because the beast will have control of all resources **(Revelation 13:17)** and tell you how and when you should get specific resources such as gas, food, housing, and water.

Nuclear War

Almost a decade ago, I had a vision where a nuke destroyed everything in its path. I woke up in a great panic because I could feel and smell the nuke as if I was there. During the end times, the world will be in a state of survival, and nations will revolt against each other **(Matthew 24:7).** I had a vision about Russia and how they will invade us and deploy nukes. I saw their military soldiers wearing civilian clothes while they studied us, living in our homes, and eventually invading us inside and out. The military soldiers for Russia that will invade us from the inside out are already here: in plain sight. Other countries will join in this invasion of the United States of America. China will partner with Russia to help bring down the USA.

CHAPTER 9
WAR WITH THE SAINTS

As a teenager, I would dream about the chaos during the reign of Anti-Christ. I was so young then and couldn't interpret those dreams, but I knew someone who could. I had a friend named Josh, whom I used to party with and hang out with, and I remember he disappeared one day. I was worried about why he had disappeared. Months went by, and I eventually gave up contacting him, but then I got a phone call from him three months later. Josh began to explain to me how God spared his life and how he went through so many complex changes, but he ended up turning his life over to God.

I didn't know what getting saved was at the time as a youth, but I noticed that the Josh I used to know was a different person. He stopped drinking and smoking and wanted to live his life for God. As Josh professed God's love and salvation, I thought sharing a recent dream with him would be a great idea because I needed interpretation. I used to keep my dreams inside, but I had to talk with someone, and I felt comfortable explaining my visions to Josh.

I told Josh about this evil man I'd seen in my vision and how he forced many to be shackled and chained together. So many people were enslaved and forced to throw their Bibles into a substantial fiery pit; as I explained my dream to him, Josh went silent momentarily.

"Dee, did you know what you just dreamed about?" asked Josh.

I said "no" to him in a curious manner.

Josh explained that I dreamt about the Antichrist, and he began explaining who the Antichrist was and his mission on Earth in the last days. I listened with both ears, but I kept thinking he could be wrong, but probably not.

As my life went on from a teen to a young adult, I remember God speaking to me and telling me about that event that I dreamt about with the burning of the bibles will occur. When I think about this event,

God told me, "They will call this event, "The Great Burning."

During this great burning, they want to burn up every doctrine about Jesus Christ and force his followers to do so.

Antichrist wants to burn a lot of Bibles because he wants the traces of God's written word eradicated from the Earth. By implementing this event called "The Great burning," he believes this would bring people to the point of no hope, making them conform.

Your relationship with God is of such great importance because, during the Great burning, they will remove the physical doctrines of Jesus. But when you have a relationship with God, there is no separation between you and him **(Romans 8:31-39)**. Therefore, learning God and his words is very important because when you read his words in the Bible, they immerse themselves in your soul.

RAPTURE

There are so many debates about the rapture. God recently gave me a dream six months ago about the rapture, and it was very disheartening to see so many people leave especially young children, and how much sorrow filled so many hearts because their loved ones were gone. Something I want to highlight about the rapture is that only valid "Christians will get rapture."

The Book of Revelation explains the Antichrist stepping on the scene, controlling many nations, and warring with the Saints. Also, it states that those here during the reign of the Antichrist must be patient, with endurance and faith. The Bible referenced them as Saints of God **(Revelation 13:8-10)**. This verse clearly states that some of God's people will be left behind, but it also says that all some inhabitants of the Earth will worship the beast, and those who worship the beast's name will be erased from the book of life. For those that may have a hard time understanding that: just because you are left behind does not mean you will be surpassed and cast aside like the non-believers.

The Bible states that Saints will be left behind during the Anti-Christ. Also, in **(Matthew 24:30-31)** the elect will see Jesus Return, and he will gather them. So, I believe that the biggest misconception is that everyone who believes in God will be raptured at the same time.

Stay strong! Whether you will gather in the clouds with God, in or before the tribulation, you must live according to God's will. If one does not get raptured, do not lose hope because he has a plan for you during this great battle.

Imprisonment

During the reign of the Antichrist, many followers of Christ were jailed or held in captivity. I had a vision many years ago where I saw so many Christians housed in jails. The reason that we were in this jail was that we didn't comply with the system that they were establishing. The was a system where they dictated our free will, and also, they tried to portray us as the root cause of all the chaos in the world.

In my vision, I saw other believers in makeshift underground cells, and the conditions were horrible. There was no bed and nothing to sit on; many people were on the floor, and I saw many people chained up together, with looks of hunger and despair painted on their faces. I remember seeing the eyes of misery on believers' faces because they felt God had abandoned them. I saw that God began to break them free by breaking down walls and crumbling buildings so they could escape.

MARTYRS

In the end, those who follow Christ will be killed and suffer great persecution because of their commitment to Christ **(Matthew 24:9).** The physical torture many believers endure is heinous and unnecessary. Many believers will suffer from death by physical mutilation. There will be those whose bodies will get dismembered. Instead of executing a quick death upon us, they would like to see us suffer, cry out and beg for pain in hopes that we would deny our Lord Jesus Christ and savior. The bloodshed of the innocent will be great in numbers. Many believers will suffer this fate because they refuse to bow down and worship the Dragon and the Beast created in his image.

MILITARY EXECUTION

For many of these things to happen to believers, they will need the power to implement them. They will search high and low for us. They know who we are. They will break down any compounds to get to us. The military soldiers will be vicious, heartless, and full of corruption. I've seen many visions where I have been running in the woods and running away from military officials. They were physically gunning down people in the middle of the streets and having no regard because they had no choice but to execute the orders given by the world leader at the time, the Antichrist. Some soldiers fear for their own lives and the lives of their families. Some soldiers will repent for their actions, and some will be with no remorse. The Devil has possessed those without remorse. These possessed soldiers will execute their orders because they think the Anti-Christ is God.

Our soldiers sworn to protect us will kill and place us in camps if we don't comply with "The New World" order.

There were going to be many checkpoints in major cities. Army soldiers are at these major checkpoints., to ensure we don't pass them. We have seen in the last five years the growth of highway tolls. They built these tolls knowing they would be a checkpoint in the beast system for every major city.

I began to see people running past these checkpoints in my visions, driving cars through them and passing the soldiers. People were climbing over fences and hiding because they knew they had just broken the martial law protocol. It was chaos at these tolls underneath the Martial law.

After we see the Antichrist rise, we know that we're about to get closer to Christ's return, but during his rise, Christians will face some of the most hellacious times on Earth that they have ever met. It will be Hell on Earth for us and many others, and the Bible tells us that they will make war with the Saints **(Revelation 13:7).** So, we must consider that being in Christ towards the End times can cost us our life, much hardship, and pain. But this hardship and pain are temporary and will not last forever. So, living in a world under the Antichrist will be disheartening because it will be painful; I do know that if God is for us, who can be against us? They will wage war against us, but we have already won. We will make it, and we will survive.

CHAPTER 10
HIS CREW

Underneath this Beast System, they desire to bring the spiritual world to the earth world. I have seen so many things in my visions that I can't explain. The level of demonic activity on Earth is unreal. I couldn't believe what I saw in my dreams from God; it was like something from a science fiction novel.

Hell is about to touch the Earth, and the Dragon and his crew will have free reign **(Revelation 13:7),** and they will wreak havoc on everyone and everything. The Dragon is so polluted that anything he touches shall be foul, and the Dragon has a significant influence on Earth that it shall be foul like him. His kingdom will manifest in the physical form. These things will happen when we know the Dragon is in full reign.

Days of Darkness

I recently had a vision that the sun didn't shine for a couple of days, and the news reporters were trying to downplay it, saying this was a random phenomenon. I knew that demons had come to possess the

Earth and its people. I tried to explain to the reporter/meteorologist that this was a bad omen and that we needed to stay indoors until these days of darkness. I began to run to the home builder store to get plywood to board up windows and aluminum foil to cover them. **(Isaiah 13:10)**

Earth Will Begin to Fade Away

I could see the sky crack open with a loud roaring sound, and the moon started falling. The moon shattered into pieces like a cookie crumbling. A sorrow filled the air, but there was a relief, too. The Earth looked like it was dying. People knew this was it; they felt they would do it all over if they had another chance, but it was too late. The end was, and is, happening before their eyes.

The Wealthy Will Hide

God allowed me to see the wealthy as they barricaded themselves in their home, thinking they were exempt from his judgment. The rich had stored their resources because they knew the end was near. They hid out below sea levels and in many other places. They don't think God will see them or wish he was looking away from them. The food and resources will rot.

God said,

"They think they will hide from me, yet they will always remain in plain sight," the resources will perish like them; they will no longer be. "

UFOs

I have seen UFOs appear during the last few years. The technology of these UFOs was something unimaginable. Now there are several sightings all over the world of those UFOs. The government will try to convince us that these are aliens and are responsible for the rapture and the things happening on Earth. God has recently revealed that these fallen angels work with our government. They knew they were here and kept this a secret for so long, and now they'll come out of hiding in the last days. They will make war with people on Earth.

Raining Fire

I remember one day, I was on the train headed to work in the morning. I was sitting on the subway seat facing the double-door window. All I could see were vast and numerous fireballs raining down through the night sky. The fireballs were like canons in their path: they were beautiful, but the beauty quickly faded because they were about to destroy Earth. I silently wept on the train because I saw what would happen to the Earth we once called our home.

CHAPTER 12
Q&A WITH GOD

What do you want people to know about this corrupt system?

The lies of Satan have drowned out this world, and his time is almost up, and forever I will reign. I wish my creation only had listened to me and followed my wise council, but instead, they allowed the enemy to drown out my voice of righteousness. My creation has shattered my emotions by living amongst the deception and failing to obey my commands. My commands were put in place to make you safe, to protect you, for you are my most important asset. I value you more than they could ever imagine. I love you where love didn't exist, I have given you my most prized possession, which is the gift of life, but my creation has allowed the enemy to come between my love and divide you from me. I have never left. I have warned you about this very moment that you currently live in. What breaks my heart: I have loved you all along, and now the enemy has taken a stronghold against my people.

God, what message do you have for the non-believers during this final hour?

There is so much evidence to prove my existence, yet they run away from it, fearing what they already know, that I am honest and alive. There are choices to be made; I have given you the will to love, the will to hate, the will to live, and the will to die. For you to choose what you may believe, that's the beauty of my choice. May your free will guide you down the path that brings you closer to me, further away from the lies and closer to the truth. If you choose the will that brings you further away from me and into the enemy's snare, remember I gave you a choice, I gave you my son, but many rejected him. I gave you my son so you shall not live in darkness but in truth and be free from lies.

What about your promises towards the Last Days for your people?

I have called my people out of the darkness. I have already ordained them for this time and moment, my dear; I promise to guide them during the end. I promise to give them hope when they don't have any, never leave or forsake them, and always advise them in this dark hour. They may suffer only for a short while, but nothing can compare to eternity with me, my dear, For I promise them that they were made for this moment, and I will ensure their life with me, for they fight and have fought hard and never gave up.

My people never sold me out. They kept my name in their mouths till the end. When my son shall arrive, they shall be crowned forever faithful. My dear, I promise my people, for I am their hope, and they are my reasons, for I adore and love them very much. I promise never to let them go in these times, my dear, but I will only hold them closer to my heart.....my dear, but I will only hold them closer to heart, and never forget them."

God, I know there will be a great battle, and this is where evil will enslave and capture us. I was wondering how this will go down.

Yes, my dear daughter, a battle will come between you versus them, and it will be an epic one, my beloved, for they will arrest you, kill many, and enslave my people. They won't relent, my child, for they are setting the stage for this to happen and using and depleting the world's resources, and they are those who are hoarding them, those I watch as they do this; they will never be able to use one drop of whatever they have stolen from my people, my dear. They will seek out my saints; they will murder innocent children till I come to take them away, my dear. They watch you at a distance, study you, and hang on the words I speak, for their payment will be triple the portion they place upon my people; I will not forget their names, and I will not remember their faces. Those who participated in taking my people captive shall reap a fate of horror. You may be killed, but there is life after death, my dear. Please know that, whatever happens, they will not taste the wine they have prepared for your bloodshed. They will taste the poisons of their eternity.

God, I know many people think this isn't the end, and they believe that life in this generation will continue and that this is just some conspiracy.

My dear, many are wise, but they seem foolish. The thoughts of man in today's world have escaped them with futile thoughts and frivolous matters. The truth is that many face a different type of reasoning and logic that isn't tested by me but through man. I have sent my son and many before and after him to warn people of this day, hoping my creation will turn their hearts to me. There is hope. It isn't too late to turn to me and away from evil.

Please don't listen to the world; the evil ones know it is time for the end to approach. They wish you not to be saved, for they know they will not be in my kingdom. I need people to heed my warning, my daughter. I have given you and many more knowledge and details about the end. This isn't a hoax... They've conspired to rule the world, not understanding that I am all-knowing. They insist on preventing my creation from knowing my name, but that is ultimately impossible, for

I am God, I have given you the Bible, I have born and raised prophets, and most importantly, I gave you my only son. He will soon return to this world he sacrificed his life for, a world that I, his father, gave him. He shall return, for he awaits my instruction, and as the days draw near, we continuously prepare, and as we design, we delay in the hope more will come to us. The world is full of evil, and it grows stronger. I can't wait any longer; I must intervene. Listen, thousands of years seem plenty to man, my dear; it almost feels never-ending to man's mind. You have only been on Earth for a short while, my beloved; you haven't been on Earth very long; it has been fading for these generations, and its time for it to end, and a new one will begin, a new life my dear, life is short, and I can't watch and feel any more pain. Jesus shall arrive soon; please change and come out from the beast system, tell them Doris tell them! I am coming. I love you so much, my dear, for these are the words that I have spoken.

THE END IS NOW; JESUS IS COMING BACK!!!!!
REPENT, AND COME OUT, THE BEAST SYSTEM!!!!

Made in the USA
Las Vegas, NV
21 September 2023

77892463R00042